Colin Powell

History Maker Bios

Laura Hamilton Waxman

Ｌ LERNER PUBLICATIONS COMPANY • MINNEAPOLIS

Illustrations by Tim Parlin

Text copyright © 2005 by Laura Hamilton Waxman
Illustrations copyright © 2005 by Lerner Publications Company

Lerner Publications Company
A division of Lerner Publishing Group
241 First Avenue North
Minneapolis, MN 55401 U.S.A.

Website address: www.lernerbooks.com

Library of Congress Cataloging-in-Publication Data

Waxman, Laura Hamilton.
    Colin Powell / by Laura Hamilton Waxman.
      p.   cm. — (History maker bios)
    Includes bibliographical references and index.
    ISBN: 0–8225–2433–3 (lib. bdg. : alk. paper)
    1. Powell, Colin L.—Juvenile literature. 2. Statesmen—United States—Biography—Juvenile literature. 3. Generals—United States—Biography—Juvenile literature. 4. African American generals—Biography—Juvenile literature. 5. United States. Army—Biography—Juvenile literature.
I. Title. II. Series.
E840.8.P64W39 2005
973.931'092—dc22
                                                  2004002595

Manufactured in the United States of America
1 2 3 4 5 6 – JR – 10 09 08 07 06 05

TABLE OF CONTENTS

INTRODUCTION   5

1. A BOY FROM THE BRONX   6

2. ARMY LIFE   14

3. WORKING IN WASHINGTON   24

4. WAR WITH IRAQ   32

5. SECRETARY OF STATE   38

TIMELINE   44

THE BUFFALO SOLDIERS   45

FURTHER READING   46

WEBSITES   46

SELECT BIBLIOGRAPHY   47

INDEX   48

INTRODUCTION

Colin Powell joined the U.S. Army when he was seventeen years old. Early on, people told him that he was the best black officer they knew. But that wasn't good enough for Colin. He wanted to be the best, period. He worked hard to prove that a black officer could be as good as the best white officer in the army.

Colin did not stop there. In the 1970s, he began working for the government in Washington, D.C. He became the first black chairman of the Joint Chiefs of Staff, the top military job in the United States. As chairman, he helped win the first war against Iraq. Colin has gone on to fight terrorism as the country's first black secretary of state. In all his jobs, he has worked hard to do his very best.

This is his story.

1 A Boy from the Bronx

Colin Luther Powell was born on April 5, 1937, to two proud parents. Luther and Maud Powell had high hopes for baby Colin and his six-year-old sister, Marilyn. Colin's parents had left their homeland of Jamaica to seek a better life in the United States.

Luther had worked his way up in the shipping department of a New York clothing company. Maud earned money sewing clothing. Both parents taught their children to work hard and have pride in everything they did.

Colin's family lived in a four-bedroom apartment on 952 Kelly Street in the Bronx in New York City. Relatives and family friends lived all along the street. Like the Powells, they sometimes struggled to make ends meet.

Colin (pronounced KOH-lihn) and his sister, Marilyn, grew up in the Bronx, New York City.

The neighbors on Kelly Street always found a way to help each other through hard times. To Colin, they were like one big family.

Just a few blocks away was Colin's elementary school. He made friends easily, but he wasn't a very good student. Studying just didn't interest him. What did interest him was World War II (1939–1945). The United States had entered the war in 1941 and fought until the war ended in 1945. Colin spent hours making model fighter planes and playing with tiny lead soldiers. He liked to direct battles on the living room rug.

Colin and his father Luther posed for this picture when Colin was in grade school. Studying did not interest young Colin much.

Colin admired World War II heroes such as these African American pilots. They were called the Tuskegee Airmen.

Colin also played games on the streets with his friends and rode around on his bicycle. One day, a furniture store owner saw him passing by. Mr. Sickser asked Colin if he wanted to earn a little money for the day. The owner needed Colin's help unloading a truck full of furniture. Colin worked hard that day, just like his parents had taught him to. The store owner was impressed. "So you're a worker," he said. "You want to come back tomorrow?" After that, Colin had a steady job.

Colin graduated from high school in February 1954. He went on to the City College of New York. Right away, he noticed that some young men in his classes wore army uniforms. He found out that they belonged to the Reserve Officer Training Corps, or the ROTC. The ROTC trains young men to be officers in the U.S. Army. ROTC members take special army classes and training workshops.

Colin liked the way those young men looked and acted. He decided to join the ROTC in the fall of 1954.

A smiling Colin stands for a picture at about the time he graduated from high school in 1954. His parents encouraged him to go to college.

CIVIL RIGHTS MOVEMENT

When Colin was a boy, black people did not have equal rights in many parts of the country. In the North, African Americans often experienced racism and unfair treatment. In the South, laws kept black and white people apart. Black people were not allowed to eat in many restaurants or stay in hotels. They had to use separate bathrooms and drinking fountains. While Colin was in college, African Americans began organizing the civil rights movement. They came together to fight for equal rights for all black citizens. They held protests and marches in cities across the country until the unfair laws and treatment began to change.

ROTC quickly became the most important part of his college life. He took pride in wearing the olive green pants and brown shirt of the ROTC uniform.

Colin did well in the Army ROTC while in college.

He also valued his close friendships with other ROTC members. These young men became part of a new family for Colin. Just like the people on Kelly Street, they would do anything for each other.

Colin trained hard and became a leader among the other ROTC students at City College. After one six-week training session, Colin received a great honor. The training officers judged him second best in the entire training camp.

Colin was thrilled. Then one sergeant pulled him aside. He said Colin would have been voted number one if he had been white. This sergeant told Colin that some army officers didn't think black and white people should be treated equally. Colin was shocked. He believed all people should have the same chance to succeed in the army. At that moment, he made a promise to himself. He would always strive to be the very best—no matter what.

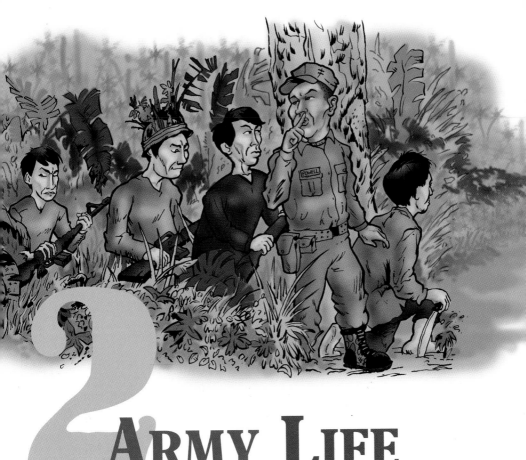

2 ARMY LIFE

In June 1958, Colin graduated from college and completed his ROTC training. He had an important choice to make. He could stay in the army and become a lieutenant, an army officer. Or he could leave the army behind for a different career.

The decision was easy for Colin. He was ready for a life in the army.

The army sent Colin to a training camp in Georgia. At Fort Benning, Colin learned to follow orders fearlessly. He also began to gain the skills he needed to lead soldiers.

Colin did well in his training and fit right in at Fort Benning. But sometimes he met people in the army who treated him differently because he was African American.

A soldier trains on a rope course at Fort Benning in Georgia. Colin began his life in the U.S. Army at the fort.

Laws separating blacks and whites made it impossible for Powell to spend time with white soldiers off the base.

Once an officer said, "Powell, you're the best black lieutenant I've ever known." Colin knew the officer meant well. But he didn't want to be compared only to other black lieutenants. Secretly, he thought, "I'm going to show you the best lieutenant in the army, period."

Life outside of the army camp caused Colin more serious problems. For the first time, he was living in the segregated South. Segregation laws kept white and black people apart. Because of these laws, Colin couldn't go to restaurants or bars with his white army buddies.

Colin thought these laws were crazy. Still, he knew he had to stay out of trouble if he wanted to do well in the army. That meant following those rules.

After five months, Colin left Georgia for his first assignment as an officer. He was going to lead a group of soldiers in Germany. U.S. soldiers had been in that country since the end of World War II.

When Colin was training in the army during the 1950s, black citizens were fighting to end segregation.

As a young lieutenant, Colin strove to be his best. His strong character earned the respect of his men.

Colin worked hard to earn the respect of his soldiers. They saw that he expected them to work as hard as he did. But he was also fair and generous. When a soldier came to him with a problem, he always tried to help. He seemed to be a natural leader.

Colin spent more than a year in Germany. After that, the army sent him to Fort Devens, Massachusetts, to command another group of soldiers.

Life at Fort Devens was not as exciting as life in Germany. But Colin liked being closer to his parents. He also liked having the time to go out on dates.

In November 1961, Colin agreed to go on a blind date with a young woman named Alma Johnson. Right away, he saw that Alma was intelligent, graceful, and beautiful. They began to spend more and more time together. Then Colin's army life got in the way.

In 1961, Colin went on a date with Alma Johnson (RIGHT). Alma was born and raised in Birmingham, Alabama. After college, she took a job in Boston, Massachusetts, not far from Fort Devens.

In the summer of 1962, Colin learned that the army was going to send him to Vietnam in Southeast Asia for a year. The people of Vietnam were at war with one another. Americans were helping one side fight against the other. Colin's job was to help train Vietnamese soldiers to be good fighters.

Before Colin left the United States, he and Alma decided to get married. They had a simple wedding on August 25. Then they moved to live near an army training camp in North Carolina. Colin would train at the camp for a few months before going to Vietnam.

A U.S. military adviser (RIGHT) helps train soldiers in Vietnam. Colin also was ordered to serve as an adviser there in 1962.

Colin and Alma Powell (CENTER) on their wedding day. They were married in Birmingham, Alabama, on August 25, 1962.

Colin and Alma were excited to begin a new life together. But they quickly ran into problems. They couldn't find a place to live. White people in North Carolina didn't want black families in their neighborhoods. The only apartments African Americans could rent were run-down and depressing. Colin and Alma didn't know what to do.

Powell served at this base in the A Shau Valley. This valley is in west-central Vietnam, along the border with Laos.

At the last minute, an army friend invited the couple to stay in his home. Colin and Alma were grateful for a nice place to live. But the unfair way they had been treated made them angry.

Just before Christmas, Colin flew to Vietnam. For the first time, he was fighting a real war. He helped a Vietnamese officer lead a group of Vietnamese soldiers in a deadly battle against enemy soldiers.

The men didn't speak much English, and Colin did not know Vietnamese. But he managed to teach them better ways to protect themselves.

Colin soon earned the respect of the Vietnamese soldiers, just as he had in Germany. Colin Powell was turning into a top-notch officer.

VIETNAM PROTESTS

A lot of Americans did not support the war in Vietnam. They saw television reports that showed the suffering of U.S. soldiers and innocent Vietnamese people. A large number of Americans wanted the fighting to stop. They began protesting the war all over the country. Many protests were peaceful. But some of them became violent, and people got hurt. The United Stated finally pulled out of the war in 1973.

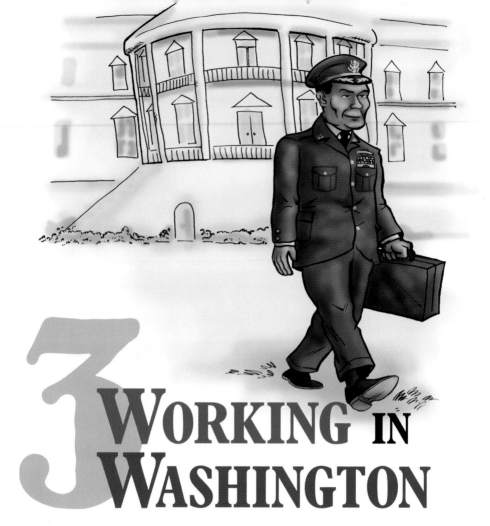

3 WORKING IN WASHINGTON

In November 1963, Colin returned home to Alma and a baby son, Michael. He also came back to many changes in the South. African Americans were winning the fight against segregation and other unfair laws.

That summer, the black leader Martin Luther King Jr. had led the March on Washington. In this protest, hundreds of thousands of people demanded equal rights for African Americans. Little by little, segregation was disappearing in the South.

Colin spent the next five years with the army in the United States. He kept his promise to himself to be the best officer possible. He also tried to be a good dad to his son, Michael, and his daughter Linda, born in 1965.

On August 28, 1963, Martin Luther King Jr. (FRONT ROW, SECOND FROM LEFT) led the March on Washington.

In the summer of 1968, the army assigned Colin to Vietnam once again. He and Alma decided to have one last special dinner together. They went to the best restaurant in town. In the past, this restaurant had shut its doors to African Americans. But with the end of segregation, Alma and Colin could eat there in style.

Colin spent an exhausting year fighting in Vietnam and then returned to the United States. He and his family moved to Washington, D.C.

In 1968, Colin had to leave Alma and their children, Michael and Linda. The army had called on him to serve again in Vietnam.

Colin (RIGHT) survived a helicopter crash while in Vietnam. He bravely helped others to escape from the aircraft.

The army paid for Colin to earn a master's degree in business at George Washington University. During his time at the university, his second daughter, Annemarie, was born.

Colin graduated in the spring of 1971. Then the army assigned him to the Pentagon, the headquarters of the nation's Department of Defense. Instead of commanding soldiers, Colin would be working in an office with government and military officials. It was a big change.

Colin worked as hard as ever and impressed his bosses at the Pentagon. The leaders of the army also noticed Colin's talent in government work. In 1972, they asked him to apply for a White House Fellowship. This fellowship would allow Colin to spend a year working for high-level White House staff. But competition for the fellowship was extremely tough. Only seventeen people would be chosen from more than one thousand applicants.

As a White House Fellow, Colin (RIGHT) met many powerful U.S. leaders, including President Richard Nixon (LEFT).

Colin wasn't sure he wanted the fellowship. He missed army life. But he followed the army's wishes and applied. He became one of only two African Americans to win the fellowship.

In the White House, Colin earned the admiration of the people he worked for. He was a fast learner, and he knew how to get a job done. Colin liked his work, but he still missed the army. In 1973, he put on his uniform once more and returned to his job as an officer.

For more than ten years, Colin went back and forth between life in the army and office work for the government. He liked being an officer best. But his bosses in Washington, D.C., kept offering him jobs.

In 1986, Colin was in Germany leading a group of seventy-five thousand soldiers. A friend and old boss from Washington, D.C., called him with a special request. He wanted Colin to come work with him for President Ronald Reagan. "We need you, Colin," he said. Colin was honored. But he didn't want to leave his post in Germany.

Four days passed, and Colin got another phone call. This time, it was from President Reagan himself. Would Colin come work for him? Colin couldn't turn down the president of the United States. "Yes, sir," he answered. "I'll do it." He left Germany for the United States at the end of 1986.

In November 1987, President Reagan asked Colin to be the country's national security adviser. He became the first African American ever to hold this important position. Colin's job was to give the president advice about the safety of the nation and about how to work with foreign countries. He became known for his intelligence, straightforward manner, and loyalty.

National Security Adviser Powell (RIGHT) speaks to President Ronald Reagan (LEFT).

Four Stars

In 1989, Colin received a great military honor. The U.S. Army made him a four-star general. Very few officers ever reach this highest rank in the military. Even fewer African Americans have been four-star generals. Once again, Colin kept his promise to be the best officer, period.

Two years later, a new president had another big job for Colin. President George H. W. Bush asked Colin to become the chairman of the Joint Chiefs of Staff, or JCS. The JCS is made up of the chiefs of the army, navy, air force, and marines. The chairman is the highest person in the JCS and the entire U.S. military. Once again, Colin became the first African American to have this job.

As chairman of the JCS, Colin was the main adviser to the president on military matters. Colin knew it would be a challenging job. But he was ready for it.

4 WAR WITH IRAQ

On the evening of August 1, 1990, the phone rang at the Powell home. A government official was calling to tell Colin some bad news. The Middle Eastern country of Iraq had just invaded a neighboring country, Kuwait.

Colin knew that the president would be worried about Iraq's leader, Saddam Hussein. Saddam was hungry for power.

He could also be ruthless. He would not treat the people in Kuwait well. And he might try to attack other Middle Eastern countries if he wasn't stopped.

President Bush decided to go to war with Iraq. He wanted to stop Saddam Hussein. Colin's job was to help the president plan the best way to win the war. Colin also worked closely with General Norman Schwarzkopf. General Schwarzkopf was going to lead the Americans in Iraq.

Colin (RIGHT), chairman of the Joint Chiefs of Staff, advises President Bush (LEFT) about going to war in Iraq.

Colin (SEATED LEFT) and General Schwarzkopf (SEATED RIGHT CENTER) talk to reporters about the 1991 war in Iraq.

The war, known as the Persian Gulf War, began on January 17, 1991. Colin was constantly on the phone getting updates and giving advice. Out of the corner of his eye, he also watched reports of the war on television. He sensed that many Americans were worried.

Colin wanted to keep the American people informed about the war. He also wanted to calm their fears.

Colin held press conferences throughout the war. At these large meetings, Colin explained what was happening in Iraq.

Powell also answered questions from reporters. Once again, he impressed people with his confidence and honesty. He earned the respect of many Americans.

Colin continued to work closely with the president and General Schwarzkopf to keep the war going smoothly. After forty-three days, the fighting ended.

IRAQ FACTS

Iraq is a small country about twice the size of Idaho. It borders the nations of Iran, Jordan, Kuwait, Saudi Arabia, Syria, and Turkey. Most of the country is desert. But Iraq also has mountains, farmland, and wet marshlands. About 25 million people live in Iraq's cities, villages, and countryside. More than 95 percent of them practice the religion of Islam.

General Powell thanks soldiers for their work during the Persian Gulf War. Colin values U.S. fighting men and women, and they respect him.

The Americans had forced the Iraqis to leave Kuwait. But Saddam Hussein stayed in power in Iraq.

Colin remained chairman of the JCS until Bill Clinton took over as president in 1993. That fall, Powell made a big change in his life. He was fifty-six years old. It was time to retire from the U.S. Army.

On September 30, Colin Powell wore his uniform for the last time. That evening, he went to a large ceremony honoring him for his service in the military. Friends, family, and politicians came to celebrate his retirement. Colin thought about all the good memories he had from his years in the army. He also thought about the promise he had made to himself long ago. He was proud that he had always worked hard to be the best officer possible.

At Colin's retirement party in 1993, U.S. military leaders thanked him for his years of service.

5 SECRETARY OF STATE

R etired General Colin Powell was famous. Many Americans wanted to hear him speak and to learn more about him. In 1995, Colin wrote a book about his life called *My American Journey*. He traveled around the country giving speeches at colleges and businesses.

Colin also talked to young people, especially young African Americans. He told them to work hard and believe in themselves.

Colin was a powerful speaker with strong opinions. Some people wondered if he might run for president. A new election was coming in 1996. Colin was very popular. His fans thought he could win.

In the end, Colin decided not to run for president. He wanted to serve his country. But he didn't think running for president was the best way for him to do it.

Colin signs copies of his book, *My American Journey*, for admirers in 1995.

Powell talks with a youngster during an America's Promise event. He helped found the community service organization in 1997.

Instead Colin devoted his time to improving the lives of children in America. In 1997, he helped start an organization called America's Promise. The organization raises money to help communities give children the skills and confidence to succeed.

In 2001, Colin's life changed again. That year, George W. Bush became president of the United States. He asked Colin to be his secretary of state.

The secretary of state is one of the president's most important advisers. This person helps the president build relationships between the United States and other nations.

Colin had enjoyed his retirement. But he agreed to return to the White House as the first black secretary of state.

Colin's new job is fast paced and demanding. He has tried to build stronger relationships with countries such as China, Russia, Pakistan, and India. He has also worked with the leaders of nations in Europe, Africa, and the Middle East.

Colin has been in the spotlight more than ever since September 11, 2001. On that day, terrorists flew airplanes into the World Trade Center in New York City and the Pentagon near Washington, D.C.

After Colin learned about the terrorist attacks on September 11, 2001, he helped decide the U.S. response to them.

Terrorists are people who use violence to frighten other people and to change countries and governments. The terrorist attacks on September 11 killed nearly three thousand people. Colin helped President Bush decide how to react to the attacks.

Since these terrorist attacks, the country has fought a war in Afghanistan and a second war in Iraq. As secretary of state, Colin's main job was not to help plan these wars.

Colin arrives in Paris, France, in 2004. As secretary of state, he often visits foreign countries.

AWARDS AND HONORS

Colin Powell has received many honors inside and outside the military. His military honors include the Bronze Star and the Purple Heart medals. Other awards he has received are the Presidential Medal of Freedom, the President's Citizens Medal, the Congressional Gold Medal, and the Secretary of State Distinguished Service Medal.

Instead, he served his country by working to get the aid and support of other nations in these wars. He has also helped the United States work together with other countries to fight terrorism.

Colin Powell has earned the respect of many Americans. He has proven that hard work and self-confidence are more important than the color of a person's skin. In the military and the government, Colin has set an example for others by doing his very best.

TIMELINE

COLIN POWELL WAS BORN
ON APRIL 5, 1937.

In the year . . .

1943 Colin's family moved into their apartment in the Bronx, New York.

1954 Colin graduated from high school and entered City College of New York. he joined the ROTC in the fall.
Age 17

1958 he graduated from college and becomes an officer in the army.

1959 he led a group of soldiers in Germany.

1962 he married Alma Johnson on August 25. he left for Vietnam in December.

1963 his son, Michael, was born.

1965 his daughter Linda was born.

1970 his daughter Annemarie was born.
Age 33

1971 he graduated from George Washington University.

1972 he began his yearlong White House Fellowship.

1987 he became the first African American national security advisor.

1989 he became the first African American chairman of the Joint Chiefs of Staff.
Age 52

1991 the first Persian Gulf War began on January 17 and ended on February 28.

1993 he retired from the army on September 30.

1995 he published his autobiography, *My American Journey.*

1997 he helped start America's Promise.

2001 he became secretary of state.
Age 64

2003 the United States went to war with Iraq on March 20.

THE BUFFALO SOLDIERS

African Americans have fought for the United States in every major war since our country's first war, the American Revolution. But many of these brave African American fighters have been forgotten. Colin Powell has helped Americans remember one group of African American soldiers known as the Buffalo Soldiers.

The Buffalo Soldiers formed in 1866. That year, the U.S. military sent several regiments, or groups, of African American soldiers to the country's western frontier. American Indians in the West called these men Buffalo Soldiers. They were impressed with the soldiers' courage and extraordinary fighting skills. Buffalo Soldier regiments went on to fight in many wars, including World War I (1914–1918) and World War II (1939–1945). Colin wanted to honor the memory of these African Americans. In 1992, he was proud to dedicate a new monument to the Buffalo Soldiers at Fort Leavenworth, Kansas.

Members of the Buffalo Soldiers, 1890

FURTHER READING

Benson, Michael. *The U.S. Army.* **Minneapolis: Lerner Publications Company, 2005.** This book examines life in the U.S. Army.

Burke, Rick. *George W. Bush.* **Chicago: Heinemann Library, 2003.** This book is a biography of the forty-third U.S. president.

Levitas, Mitchel, ed. *A Nation Challenged: A Visual History of September 11 and Its Aftermath.* **Young Reader's Edition. New York: Scholastic, 2002.** Read newspaper excerpts and see photographs recording the terrorist attacks that occurred in New York City and Washington, D.C.

Price Hossell, Karen. *The Persian Gulf War.* **Chicago: Heinemann Library, 2003.** Read about the events before and during the 1991 war with Iraq.

Schafer, Christopher. *Attack in Iraq.* **Minneapolis: Abdo & Daughters, 2003.** This book describes the most recent war against Saddam Hussein and his government in Iraq.

Venable, Rose. *The Civil Rights Movement.* **Chanhassen, MN: Child's World, 2002.** Read about the civil rights struggle in the United States during the 1960s.

WEBSITES

America's Promise
http://www.americaspromise.org/
Learn about the organization Colin Powell founded to help America's young people.

Buffalo Soldier Monument
http://leav-www.army.mil/pao/buffalo/
Find photographs of the monument, along with links to articles about the history of the Buffalo Soldiers.

Secretary of State Colin L. Powell
The White House
http://www.whitehouse.gov/government/powell-bio.html
Read information about Colin Powell on the White House's official website.

SELECT BIBLIOGRAPHY

Adler, Bill. *The Generals: The New American Heroes.* New York: Avon Books, 1991.

Chen, Edwin. "The Presidential Transition; Bush to Set Tone with His First Pick: Colin Powell." *Los Angeles Times,* December 16, 2000, A-1.

Harari, Oren. *The Leadership Secrets of Colin Powell.* New York: McGraw-Hill, 2002.

Means, Howard. *Colin Powell: Soldier/Statesman— Statesman/Soldier.* New York: Donald I. Fine, 1992.

Powell, Colin. *My American Journey.* New York: Ballantine Books, 1995.

Roth, David. *Sacred Honor: A Biography of Colin Powell.* Grand Rapids, MI: Zondervan Publishing House, 1993.

Woodward, Bob. *The Commanders.* New York: Simon & Schuster, 1991.

INDEX

America's Promise, 40

Buffalo Soldiers, 45
Bush, George H. W., 31, 33
Bush, George W., 40, 42

City College of New York, 10
civil rights (also equal rights),
    11, 13, 25
Clinton, Bill, 36

Fort Benning, Georgia, 15
Fort Devens, Massachusetts,
    18–19

Germany, 17–19, 29

Hussein, Saddam, 33, 36

Iraq, 5, 32–36, 42

Joint Chiefs of Staff, 5, 31

King, Martin Luther Jr., 25

My American Journey, 38, 39

national security adviser, 30
New York City, 6, 41

Nixon, Richard, 28

Pentagon, 27–28
Powell, Alma Johnson (wife),
    19, 20–22, 24, 26
Powell, Annemarie
    (daughter), 27
Powell, Linda (daughter), 25, 26
Powell, Luther (father), 6–7, 8
Powell, Marilyn (sister), 6, 7
Powell, Maud (mother), 6–7
Powell, Michael (son), 24, 25,
    26

Reagan, Ronald, 29–30
Reserve Officer Training
    Corps (ROTC), 10–13, 14
retirement, 37

Schwarzkopf, Norman 33, 34, 35
secretary of state, 5, 40–43
segregation, 11, 16–17, 21, 25
September 11, 2001, 41–42

Vietnam, 20, 22–23, 26, 27

Washington, D.C., 5, 26, 29
White House, 28–29, 41
World War II, 8, 9, 17, 45

Acknowledgments
The images in this book are used with the permission of: © William Philpott/
Reuters/CORBIS, p. 4; Tim Parlin, pp. 6, 14, 24, 32, 38, 44; © CORBIS SYGMA,
pp. 7, 8, 10, 12, 18, 19, 21, 26, 27, 28, 37; courtesy of Library of Congress, pp. 9,
(LC-F9-02-4503-330-5 (8-6), 45 (LC-USZC4-6161); © Hulton-Deutsch Collection/
CORBIS, p. 15; © CORBIS, pp. 16, 36; © Bettmann/CORBIS, p. 17, 20, 22; courtesy
of the National Archives, p. 25; courtesy of the Ronald Reagan Presidential Library,
p. 30; courtesy of the George H. W. Bush Presidential Library, p. 33; courtesy of the
Defense Visual Information Center, p. 34; © Tom Horan/CORBIS SYGMA, p. 39;
© J. Allen Hansley/ZUMA Press, p. 40; © Reuters/CORBIS, p. 41; © Getty Images,
p. 42. **Front cover:** © Getty Images; illustrations by Tim Parlin. **Back cover:** courtesy
of the Library of Congress (LC-USW361-952). **For quoted material:** pp. 9, 16, 29, 30,
Colin Powell, My American Journey (New York: Ballantine Books, 1995).